W9-CHE-592

WHERE DOES GARBAGE GO?

BY ISAAC ASIMOV

Gareth Stevens Children's Books
MILWAUKEE

For a free color catalog describing Gareth Stevens' list of high-quality children's books, call 1-800-341-3569 (USA) or 1-800-461-9120 (Canada).

Library of Congress Cataloging-in-Publication Data

Asimov, Isaac
    Where does garbage go? / by Isaac Asimov. — A Gareth Stevens Children's Books ed.
       p. cm. — (Ask Isaac Asimov)
    Includes bibliographical references and index.
    Summary: Briefly examines how we get rid of the things we throw away, describing
some of the problems of waste disposal and some of the solutions.
    ISBN 0-8368-0742-1
    1. Refuse and refuse disposal—Juvenile literature. 2. Recycling (Waste, etc.)—Juvenile
literature. [1. Refuse and refuse disposal.] I. Title. II. Series: Asimov, Isaac, 1920-
Ask Isaac Asimov.
TD792.A85 1991
363.72'8—dc20   91-50361

A Gareth Stevens Children's Books edition

Edited, designed, and produced by
Gareth Stevens Children's Books
1555 North RiverCenter Drive, Suite 201
Milwaukee, Wisconsin 53212, USA

Picture Credits
pp. 2-3, © Gareth Stevens, Inc., 1991/Ken Novak; pp. 4-5, © W. S. Paton/Bruce Coleman Limited; pp. 6-7, © Michael Yamashita; pp. 8-9, © Tony Souter/Hutchison Library; pp. 10-11, © Natalino Fenech/Bruce Coleman Limited; pp. 12-13, Kurt Carloni/Artisan, 1991; pp. 14-15, Rick Karpinski/DeWalt and Associates, 1991; p. 14 (inset), © William Meyer/Third Coast; pp. 16-17, © Karen A. Sherlock/Third Coast; pp. 18-19, Kurt Carloni/Artisan, 1991; pp. 20-21, © Dr. Eckart Pott/Bruce Coleman Limited; pp. 22-23, © Herbert Kranawetter/Bruce Coleman Limited; p. 24, © Herbert Kranawetter/Bruce Coleman Limited

Cover photograph, © Gareth Stevens, Inc., 1991/Ken Novak: From banana peels to old tennis shoes, from disposable spoons to drinking straws, our garbage is piling up and polluting the Earth.

Series editor: Elizabeth Kaplan
Series designer: Sabine Beaupré
Picture researcher: Diane Laska
Consulting editor: Matthew Groshek

Printed in MEXICO

3 4 5 6 7 8 9 98 97 96

Contents

Words that appear in the glossary are printed in **boldface** type the first time they occur in the text.

Exploring Our Environment

Look around you. You see forests, fields, lakes, and rivers. You see farms, factories, houses, and cities. All of these things make up our **environment**. Sometimes there are problems with the environment. For example, the garbage that we produce pollutes our land, our water, and even our air. Where does all this garbage come from? Where does it go? Why is it harmful? Let's find out.

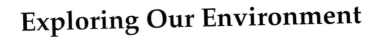

All the Things We Throw Away

Think about all the things you throw out every day. An empty cereal box. A used-up toothpaste tube. The plastic wrapper from a new box of pencils. An apple core from lunch. Chicken bones from dinner. All this stuff and more ends up in your garbage can.

Your neighbors up and down the block fill their garbage cans with the same sorts of trash. Once a week, a big truck comes and hauls it all away. What happens to all of this garbage?

7

Dumping, Burning, Burying

In some communities, the garbage is dumped into the ocean. In other communities, it is burned in a big furnace called an **incinerator**. In many communities, the garbage ends up in a **landfill**. At the landfill, garbage is spread out in layers on the ground. Then it is mashed down by a huge machine and covered over with dirt. Layers of garbage are mounded and shaped into rolling hills. In time, the site of the landfill can be made into a park. Trees and grass are planted over the old piles of garbage.

9

Out of Sight, But Not Out of Mind

For many years, people dumped, burned, or buried garbage without thinking twice. But in recent years, people have come to see that getting rid of garbage is just not that easy.

Garbage dumped into the oceans sometimes washes back to shore. Then the beaches have to be closed and cleaned up. Burning garbage pollutes the air. As garbage is burned, dangerous chemicals, including **lead** and **mercury**, go up in the smoke. If leftover ashes from the burned garbage are buried, harmful chemicals in the ashes pollute the land.

11

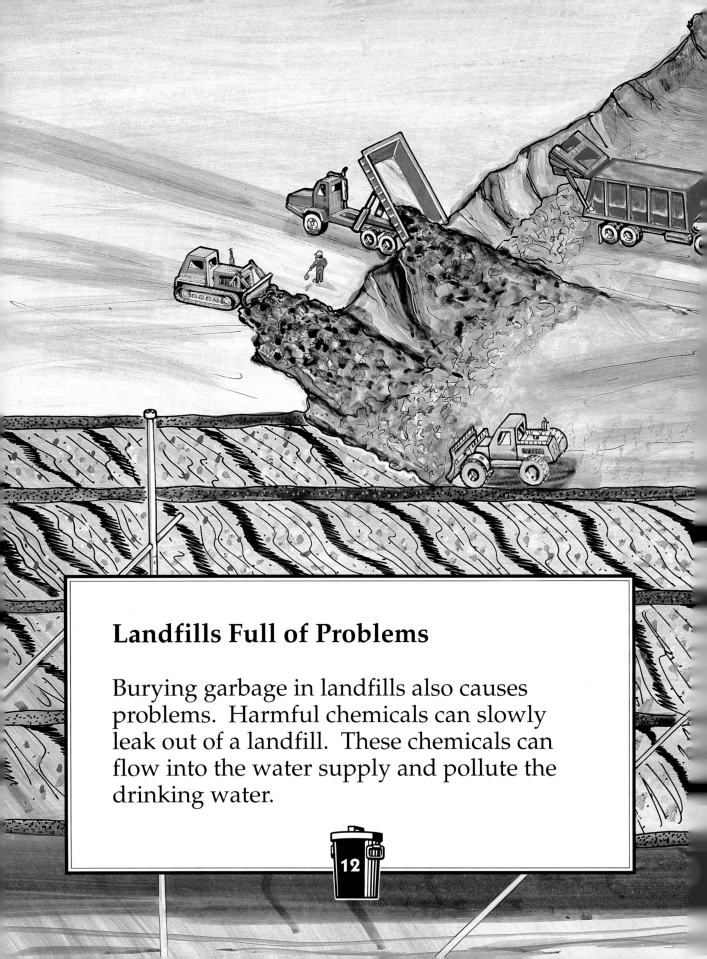

Landfills Full of Problems

Burying garbage in landfills also causes problems. Harmful chemicals can slowly leak out of a landfill. These chemicals can flow into the water supply and pollute the drinking water.

12

Many new landfills have been built to prevent harmful chemicals from leaking out. In these landfills, a layer of plastic lines the entire area where garbage is dumped. But even these landfills don't solve all the problems. They are filling up so fast that we soon won't have any place to put all our garbage.

Danger! Toxic Wastes

Ordinary garbage causes enough problems.
But hospitals, factories, and other businesses
sometimes produce garbage that can cause
serious diseases and slowly poison the
environment. These wastes are called **toxic
wastes**. Chemicals left over from some
pesticides and plastics are toxic wastes.
People working with the chemicals have to
wear special protective clothing. **Radioactive**
wastes from nuclear power plants, hospitals,
and science laboratories pose extreme danger.
And so far, no one has found a safe way to
dispose of many of these toxic wastes.

nuclear power plant

hospital

science laboratory

factory

factory

paint factory

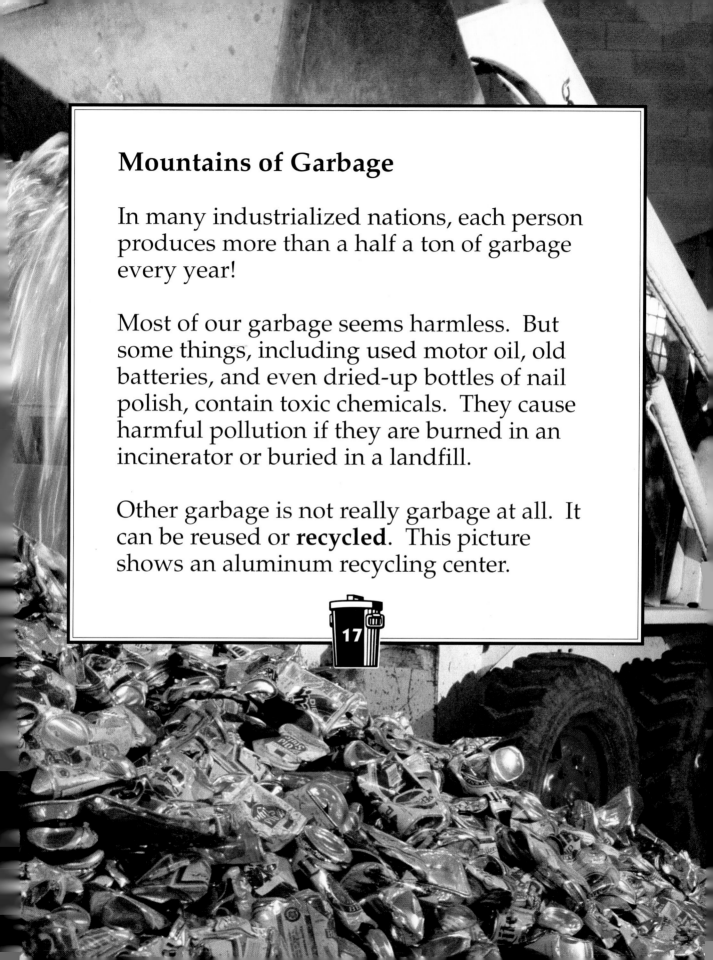

Mountains of Garbage

In many industrialized nations, each person produces more than a half a ton of garbage every year!

Most of our garbage seems harmless. But some things, including used motor oil, old batteries, and even dried-up bottles of nail polish, contain toxic chemicals. They cause harmful pollution if they are burned in an incinerator or buried in a landfill.

Other garbage is not really garbage at all. It can be reused or **recycled**. This picture shows an aluminum recycling center.

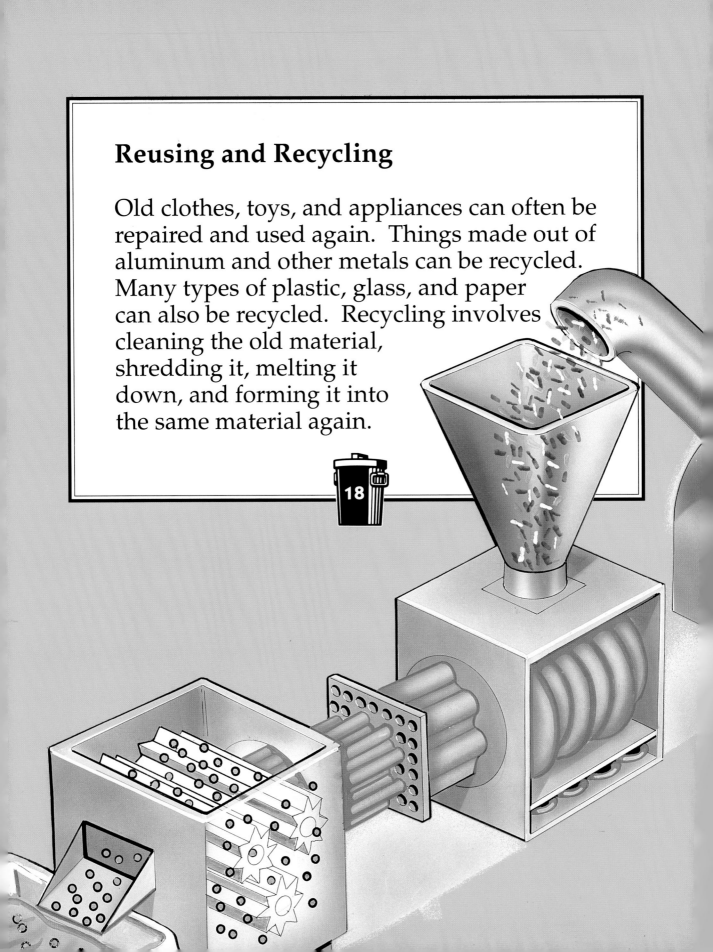

Reusing and Recycling

Old clothes, toys, and appliances can often be repaired and used again. Things made out of aluminum and other metals can be recycled. Many types of plastic, glass, and paper can also be recycled. Recycling involves cleaning the old material, shredding it, melting it down, and forming it into the same material again.

18

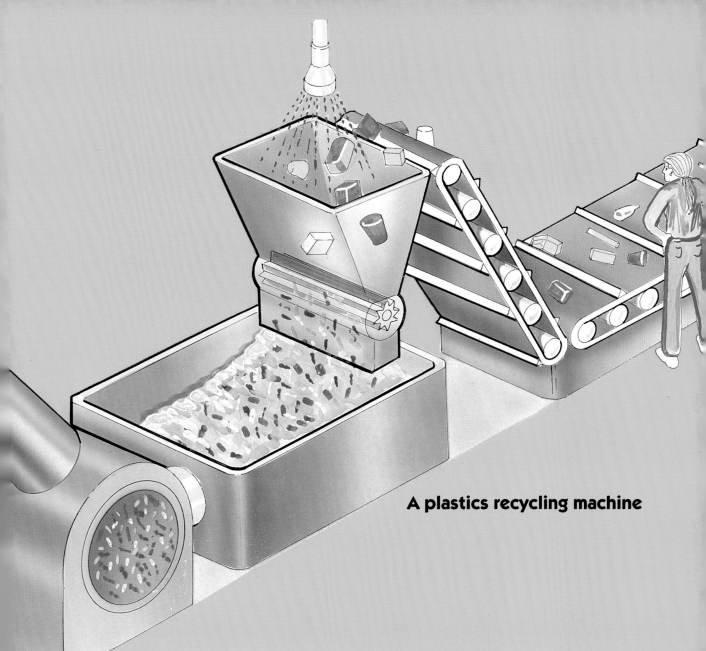

A plastics recycling machine

Composting is a way of recycling food scraps and yard wastes. When mixed with layers of soil, these materials break down, or **decompose**, and enrich the soil.

Starting at Home

You can help solve the garbage problem by throwing out less. Set up recycling bins for your family to separate paper, plastics, glass, aluminum, and other metals from your regular garbage. Get someone to help you take these materials to a recycling center if your town or city doesn't pick them up for you. Try not to waste paper — use scrap paper for notes or gift wrap. If you have a yard, you can start a compost pile in your garden with food and yard wastes that will enrich the soil.

20

Every Little Bit Helps

The mountains of garbage we have produced won't disappear overnight. But we can all help improve the environment by producing less garbage. The land, air, and water will stay cleaner. Health risks from harmful chemicals will be reduced. Bit by bit, we can make our world a better place for everyone.

More Books to Read

Why Is the Air Dirty? by Isaac Asimov (Gareth Stevens)
Garbage: Our Endangered Planet by Karen O'Connor (Lucent Books)
Too Much Garbage by Patricia Lauber (Garrard)
Trash! by Charlotte Wilcox (Lerner)

Places to Write

Here are some places you can write to for more information about garbage and recycling. Be sure to tell them exactly what you want to know about. Give them your full name and address so that they can write back to you.

Household Hazardous Waste
   Project
1031 East Battlefield, Suite 214
Springfield, Missouri 65807

Institute of Scrap Recycling
   Industries, Inc.
1627 K Street NW, 7th Floor
Washington, D.C. 20006

Greenpeace Foundation
185 Spadina Avenue, 6th Floor
Toronto, Ontario M5T 2C6

Glossary

composting (KAHM-post-ing): recycling food scraps and yard wastes by mixing them with layers of soil; these wastes help enrich the soil.

decompose (dee-kuhm-POZE): to break down chemically; food scraps and yard wastes decompose when they are mixed with soil.

environment (en-VIE-run-ment): the natural and artificial things that make up the Earth.

incinerator (in-SIN-uh-ray-tuhr): a furnace for burning garbage.

landfill: a garbage disposal site where garbage is spread out in layers, compacted, and covered with dirt. Eventually trees can be planted on a landfill and the area can be made into a park.

lead (LED): a dull, soft, poisonous metal.

mercury (MER-kyuh-ree): a silvery white, poisonous metal that is used in thermometers and batteries.

pesticide (PEHS-tih-side): a chemical put on plants to kill insects.

radioactive (RAY-dee-oh-ACK-tihv): having the property of giving off harmful atomic particles; exposure to radioactive wastes can cause serious diseases.

recycle (ree-SIE-kuhl): to clean and melt down or shred a material so that it can be made into the same material again.

toxic waste: any waste that can cause serious disease and poison the environment.

Index